Ken Alley

AWKWARD CHRISTIAN SOLDIERS

AWKWARD

KEN ALLEY P.K.

CHRISTIAN SOLDIERS

Harold Shaw Publishers
Wheaton, Illinois

ISBN 0-87788-024-7

Edited by Elizabeth Cody Newenhuyse
Cover illustration and inside cartoons copyright © 1998 by Mary Chambers
Cover design by David LaPlaca

Library of Congress Cataloging-in-Publication Data

Awkward Christian soldiers : comic relief from the back pew / [edited] by Ken Alley.

     p.   cm.
   ISBN 0-87788-024-7
   1. Christianity—Humor. 2. Christianity—Anecdotes. 3. Church—Humor. 4. Church—Anecdotes.
   I. Alley, Ken.
  PN6231.C35A95 1998
  200—dc21   97-43536
                                          CIP

02 01 00 99 98

10 9 8 7 6 5 4 3 2 1

Dedicated to my parents,
Joe and Bettye Alley,
who taught the Christian life by living it . . .
and laughing a lot.

Contents

Introduction

Because of my years of being a Preacher's Kid (PK) and routinely getting hauled out of church by my mother for laughing out loud, I *knew* funny things happened in church.

Encouraged by God's own sense of humor (listen to how he made some people sing), I began to collect stories from family, friends, and patients. Listening and watching as they recalled their own funny, fond memories, I saw the value of laughing at ourselves, even in the most pious situations.

Advertising my interest in funny anecdotes in national church magazines produced many stories from all over the country. *Awkward Christian Soldiers* (which, in truth, we all are) is an effort to share the fun of being human. Funny things that happen to real people produce the best laughs of all. Jokes are great, but life can be hilarious just as it happens.

Humorous stories about all aspects of life continue to come in. Going to the mailbox is one of the highlights of my day. I'm counting on the old memories, and the ones not yet made, to provide me with new collections for years to come!

Enjoy!

Frankenstein, Tarzan, and the Five New Convicts;
or, "Did the Pastor Really Say <u>That?</u>"

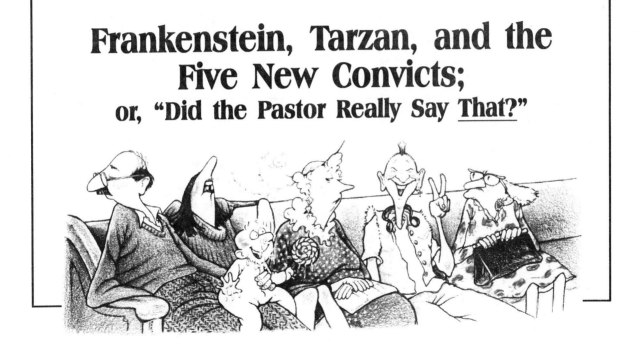

A young man who had just finished seminary came to preach for us one Sunday. He told us that one of the ways the students practiced speaking was to put a dozen marbles in their mouths. As they progressed, they were allowed to get rid of a marble every so often. When they lost all their marbles, they were ready to become preachers.

M.L., CA

The first time I ever stepped into the pulpit, I had just opened my mouth to say the very first word of my sermon when there was a brilliant flash of lightning, a deafening roll of thunder, and the power went out. You could say I was a bit intimidated.

B.H., NE

Time after time a well-meaning preacher would pray publicly, "Lord, be with those who are sick of us." Finally someone took him aside and suggested that he pray, "Be with those who are sick among us."

M.G., KS

One Sunday as our pastor was praying for the sick in our congregation, he said, "And God, especially be with . . . uh—

uh—uh . . . You know who I mean." He had forgotten their names.

T.A., MN

On a recent Sunday our minister said in a sermon on Matthew 6, "In his letter, Jesus wrote . . ." I didn't know Jesus wrote any letters.

S.E., CT

As a young preacher before the video camera in sermon delivery class, I took Matthew 4 as my text. Coming to verse 5, I got my "tang tongueled" and said, "Then the devil took him into the holy city; and he had him stand on the TEN-TACLE of the PIMPLE!" Try to imagine that one.

J.L., OK

I was trying to make a point that lack of communication is the major cause of divorce, but somehow things got mixed up and I said "marriage" was the main cause of divorce.

M.S., TX

I did a funeral once and said the deceased "died of death."

A.S., MN

An elder was speaking to the congregation, comparing a mother's tender love for her infant son to God's love for us. He said, "She bathes him and boils him in oil."

B.A., CA

Preaching from:

Matthew 5: "A hill set on a city cannot be hid."

Matthew 12: "As Jonah was in the welly of the bell."

Matthew 2: "They offered unto him gifts, gold, and Frankenstein."

R.C., AZ

During a confirmation service, referring to the new converts, the pastor asked for the five new "convicts" to come to the front of the church. He never knew what he said, but several people had to leave the building because they were laughing so hard.

L.U., NE

I was at a church picnic and the pastor, who loved to eat, asked if I had brought my coconut cream pie (his favorite). I told him no, that I hadn't had time to make one. He said, "That's okay, I still love you. Not as much, but I still love you."

"They offered unto Him gifts, gold, and Frankenstein."

I'm not sure, but I think he was serious.

E.B., KS

The preacher was thrilled, as a man he had worked with a long time came forward to be baptized. The man was six-foot-four and about 240 pounds. As the preacher lifted him out of the baptismal water, he felt his back go out. The faithful new Christian's first act was to carry his pastor out of the water.

V.D., OK

While in a Bible class, the minister announced, "Tonight's lesson is 'Money Doesn't Buy Happiness.'" Having been unemployed for some time, I thought out loud, "No, but it sure makes your misery more tolerable." The preacher replied, "Boy, you just ruined my whole lesson."

M.G., KS

I heard a burned-out preacher say, "I love the church, it's the brethren I can't stand!"

S.B. OR

I was listening to a sermon that made reference to sports stars and the preacher referred to Michael Jordan as

Michael Jackson. Another time, she spoke of the great basketball player "Magic Bird."

The preacher was so caught up in the drama of his presentation concerning the Crucifixion that he said, "And Mary looked up at Jesus and said, 'My God, my God, why hast thou forsaken me?'" Then he said, "I'm sorry, Mary didn't say that. Jesus did. I mean Jesus said that to God." He started over.

A.B. KS

In my pastor's opening remarks last Sunday, he said that every day is a new day: "We all make decisions from the moment we get up. We decide whether to have breakfast or not. We decide what shoes to wear. We decide whether to wear pants or a skirt—well, women can decide that anyway—because most men don't wear skirts . . . at least those who belong to this church . . . I hope. I, uh, probably should continue with my sermon before I get in more trouble."

D.M., AZ

As I awoke during a sermon the pastor said, "Where the Scriptures speak, we speak. Where the Scriptures are silent, we sleep."

S.B., AR

Instead of saying the prodigal son ate "with the hogs," the preacher said the prodigal son ate "like a hog."

R.L., TN

I heard of a preacher referring to the Cross as the "Big T" and to Jesus and the apostles as "JC and the Boys."

S.C. NE

The sermon was about throwing all your alcoholic beverages into the river. The next song was "Shall We Gather at the River?"

P.N., OR

My daddy tells of the time the preacher was sternly and loudly declaiming the evils of alcohol. For support he called on a lady who was a pillar of the congregation. "Don't you agree, Sister Anne?" he exclaimed.

"Oh, actually I enjoy a little toddy once in a while," came the quiet reply of the elderly saint.

While talking about parents letting go of the apron strings, the speaker said "overproductive parents" instead of "overprotective" parents.

M.W., NE

Our pastor meant to say, "We all know how tough childrearing can be." What came out of his mouth was, "We all know how tough child*bearing* can be." The mothers in the congregation thought, *You don't know the half of it.*

P.S., AL

While describing the newest addition to a family, the preacher said, "The baby weighed eighteen pounds and was seven inches long."

A.K., WA

I was the youngest PK in my family for thirteen years. One night when Mom was at her nursing job, my older brother and I sat down with Dad to play a game. Just before we began, Dad said, in his best Ronald Reagan impersonation, "Well . . . well . . . well . . . your mother is pregnant!" I was thrilled that I would soon have a live doll to play with. My brother's reaction was a bit more cynical. His comment was, "I didn't think you guys did it anymore."

Parents are human—even when your parents are the pastor and his wife! So when people ask, "What is it like, growing up in a parsonage?" I have to chuckle.

B.R., NE

During a revival, the evangelist asked that all Christians come forward to pray with the "seekers." He meant to say, "except for those who have a baby in their lap or are holding one in their arms," but what came out was, "Unless you are having a baby."

E.T., IN

My pastor was talking about all the years Enoch lived but kept referring to him as "Eunuch."

Twin sisters were being received into membership at a local church and they were introduced as the "sin twisters."

D.S., AZ

Trying to be creative, I started "advertising" my next sermon on the Second Coming of Christ. I had little signs taped on doors, ceilings, the sidewalk, and so on, that said, "He's Coming!" In my enthusiasm, I got a clever idea of sending every family of the congregation a note (which had no return address) that simply said, "He's Coming!" I imagined that all I had to do on Sunday was step into the pulpit and say, "In case you haven't heard, He's coming!" However, my joke lost its effectiveness when one of the widows who had received my card became concerned and called the police.

R.W., IL

With a sermon on "Some Things for a Christian to Remember" on my mind, I turned on the water to fill the baptistry, which was directly behind the pulpit. Turning it on and off required a trip downstairs to the other end of the building, and it had no overflow valve. As I began, "This morning I want you to remember . . . " I heard the splashing of water behind me. Immediately it dawned on me what I had done. "Oh,

no, I didn't remember to turn off the water in the baptistry! Someone turn it off, quick!" Some believed I had planned the whole thing.

R.W., IL

When I was in seminary many years ago, our professor of worship and preaching impishly warned us to be careful in reading the King James Version of Ephesians 6:16 containing the phrase, "the fiery darts of the wicked," lest we get caught in an unfortunate Spoonerism (think about it). One of my fellow students was leading chapel on a day when the Epistle lesson came from that text, and he panicked over making the blunder the professor had warned us against.

Naturally, as so often happens when we bend over backward *not* to make a mistake, we fall right in . . . which is what happened to the poor guy. Out came the dreaded words. The chapel congregation burst out laughing. That was nearly fifty years ago, but I still can't read that passage in public—even in modern translations—without breaking into a grin.

R.G., WI

At our church, a special plea was given about the never-ending heat. The preacher started the prayer by exclaiming, "God, it's hot!" We knew what he meant, but it didn't come out quite the way he intended.

L.L. FL

The shortest prayer I ever heard a preacher pray was "Dear God, you know our thoughts. Amen."

C.N., ND

Our pastor's wife was leading a serious discussion when her miscue lightened the mood. She said, "As for me, I will serve man, not God."

The preacher, walking slowly up to the podium, said, "Woke up with a nag this morning." What he meant was he woke up with a nagging backache, but the congregation cut loose.

M.S., AR

The lesson topic was earthly possessions and how we put too much value on them. My husband was listing some of these possessions, such as money, fancy homes, recreational toys, and even living possessions such as pets. He said, "Yes, even our pets can sometimes have more value than they should. But what am I talking about, when I sleep with a dog!" Suddenly there was a heavy silence. He thought to himself, *I wonder if anyone thinks I was referring to my wife?* He cautiously looked across the room and there were a couple of people holding in explosive laughs. He quickly said, "No, no, I don't mean my wife, I mean Jo Jo, our dog!" Too late.

G.O., MT

During a panel discussion about how important pastors' wives were in their husbands' ministries, one preacher said, "Any woman who wants to be a preacher's wife should be committed" . . . pause . . . "er, should be dedicated."

C.M., AR

The pastor's wife fell asleep in the middle of her husband's sermon. Her head lolled back and her mouth opened up wide, causing her jaws to lock. The preacher had to stop what he was doing to help his wife shut her mouth.

S.M., FL

An evangelist who was about six feet, three inches tall was known for her long prayers when approaching the Lord about the needs of the congregation. She would go on and on and on with general pleas, to the point that many people would just quit praying and open their eyes, look around, and entertain themselves.

When she finally got to petitioning God for the specific needs of people, she said, "And now, Lord, we beseech thee for those who really need help." Her husband, a five-foot-five baker, raised his hand for everybody to see and pointed at her.

D.D., MO

My father, a retired pastor, was visiting from out of state. He was having a "grandfatherly" time with my little ones, playing catch, reading them stories, tucking them into bed. We were all really glad to see him. On Sunday we went to church and he was asked to lead the congregation in the Lord's Prayer. He ascended to the pulpit and asked all to bow their heads and join him in this prayer. He started off, "Now I lay me down to sleep, I pray the Lord my soul to keep. . . ." Everyone laughed, but understood his absent-mindedness.

G.G., NE

In my church it is customary for the person who presides at the Communion service to say a few words about the Crucifixion or read a Bible passage about the Cross. One Sunday, an older gentleman in charge talked so long about the death, burial, and resurrection of Jesus, one could have mistaken it for the sermon. After about twelve minutes and many squirming listeners, he finally finished and proceeded with the Communion.

After this, as the pastor got up to preach, he said, with a note of gentle reproach, "Well, since _____ already used up half my time, I'll only give you two of the four points in my sermon."

A.K., WA

A few years ago, I was asked to be a guest speaker at a neighboring church. I met with the liturgist in the pastor's study, put on my robe, and with much dignity took my place at the front of the sanctuary. When it came time for my reading of the Scriptures, I stood and flipped my mike cord out of the way as I walked to the lectern. Halfway there, my left leg refused to come along because the cord did a half-hitch around my ankle. It was too late to act as if nothing had happened, so I very carefully removed the obstacle.

Since this act was definitely not in the order of worship, I improvised by saying, "It is very evident to me you folks have a line on the preacher."

O.R., IN

On a live television interview, the subject was forgiveness, and the text was the familiar Romans 3:23, "for all have sinned and fall short of the glory of God." One of the panel said, "Thanks be to God who delivers us from our falling shorts."

H.B., OK

Arriving at the gravesite, I recited the Twenty-third Psalm. A dear friend, there to assist me, began his prayer, "Will you prease play with me?—uh—will you play with me prease?—uh, bow your heads!"

J.D., KY

One of our elders died and I was trying to convey the thought that those of us who are younger owe a great debt to the older soldiers who have "blazed the trail." I said, "who have trazed the blails," "trailed the blaze," then finally, "blailed the trazes." Whereupon I went on to something I could pronounce, like the benediction.

J.D., KY

I was at a funeral where the priest was delivering the eulogy. He went on and on about how good the deceased was, what a terrific mother she was, whose kids were always clean and so well behaved, etc. The only problem was, I knew the deceased, and she didn't have any children.

C.N., NE

Our minister's name is Bruce Goodwin. In the bulletin's order of worship, he was listed as "Bruck" Goodwin. It was an obvious typo, and, humorist that he is, Bro. Goodwin couldn't let it go. When he got up to the pulpit to deliver his sermon he said, "I know everyone was excited to hear my brother Bruck speak, but due to unforeseen circumstances, he can't be here today as the bulletin announced, so I will be giving the sermon as usual."

K.A., NE

During the sermon our pastor was telling a story where one character quite forcefully tells another to "SIT DOWN!" As the preacher shouted these words, he startled an elderly lady at the back of the church who had just stood up, presumably to go out to the ladies' room.

During the time of prayer for members of the congregation, we were praying for Bill W., who was awaiting the results of his biopsy. The pastor actually ended up praying that the results of Bill's "autopsy" would be favorable.

The pastor was praying for an elderly lady in the congregation who had taken a bad fall and was in the hospital. She had fallen down a flight of fourteen stairs, but when Pastor was praying for her, he said that she'd fallen down fourteen *flights* of stairs. My husband got one of those attacks of giggles when he pictured someone tumbling down all those steps like a cartoon character.

My father was leading a service in a small town in northern Indiana, where the former governor of the state—a Republican—was a regular churchgoer. My dad was using as his text the story of the Pharisee and the publican. But out of Dad's mouth came the Scripture, "But the Republican would not so much as lift his eyes up unto heaven."

A.M., OH

Our Christmas service started with the youth minister and some of the children singing carols. While delivering the sermon, which was about the birth, death, and resurrection of Christ, he came to the baptism of Jesus and said ever so sincerely, "and the Holy Spirit descended from heaven in the form of a turtledove." He promptly realized his blooper and decided to finish it with a bang, saying, "No, make that two turtledoves and a partridge in a pear tree!"

J.H., WA

One of the worst blizzards of the year hit one Sunday morning. I certainly didn't expect anyone to show up for church. But one hardy farmer trudged his way to the front door of the church, came in and sat down. Well, by golly, since he had gone to all that trouble to come to church, I was going to give him my sermon, in all its splendor. After I was finished he said, "Thanks for the sermon, Pastor, but you know, if I just had one cow come home, I'd feed her, but I wouldn't give her the whole bale of hay."

J.S., NE

There was a beautiful formal wedding one Sunday afternoon. The minister was a bit hard of hearing. When the time came for the vows to be said, he asked the bride, "Do you take this man . . ." She answered, "I do."

Silence. The minister instructed her to answer, "I do."

She said, "I did."

"No," said the poor parson, "the answer is, 'I do.'"

Very clearly the bride replied, "I *did* say I do." By then most of the guests were dissolving in laughter.

F.P., TN

Right after the "I dos" in our wedding ceremony, the old priest unfolded a beautiful white napkin—one I assumed he usually used in our Communion service. He proceeded to honk his nose in it so loudly that all in attendance cracked up laughing.

A.F., NE

The young pastor was beaming, as were the bride and groom before him. All had gone well with this, his first wedding. While waiting for the recessional to begin, he leaned over to ask the bride if she wanted to kiss. With that, she reached over the altar rail, gave the pastor a kiss, then took her bridegroom by the arm and marched out—leaving behind a very red-faced young preacher.

D.W., MN

At a recent wedding the groom was late. Turning on my portable mike, I headed out to announce to the congregation that the groom had been contacted and that the wedding would take place in another fifteen minutes. In the hall I met the custodian and photographer and said couples should pay more attention to wedding times than to flowers. This was fine, except my mike was on and the congregation also overheard the custodian complaining about the lateness of the wedding and his other obligations. So I announced to the custodian, "We should get time and a half for this wedding!" Then I proceeded to say, "I have enough time; I'm going to the bathroom." At the sound of rushing water, one of the parishioners ran down the aisle and yelled into the bathroom, "Your mike is on!" The most painful part of this experience was having to face all those people with their huge grins when the groom did arrive and the wedding finally began.

J.L., CT

One pastor proclaimed, "I now pronounce you male and female."

One evening at church, all the flowers that had been used for a wedding earlier in the day were placed by the pulpit. Right in the middle of the sermon, a bumblebee came buzzing out of one of the flowers. Needless to say, the preacher lost his train of thought.

A.S., MI

While I was baptizing a child more than thirty years ago, a little feather detached from a pigeon flying outside and came floating in through an open window. It landed on the baptismal font, quite symbolic of the baptism of Christ when the Holy Spirit descended on him like a dove. The family still has the feather.

C.N., PA

The pastor was talking about Simon Peter and his relationship with Jesus when, without realizing it, he referred to the disciple as "Simple Simon."

H.A., NH

Our minister's sermon topic was Samson and Delilah. Throughout the entire message, however, he kept calling Samson "Tarzan."

I fell asleep listening to a tape of my own sermon.

F.L., MA

The preacher's sermon topic was Samson—but he kept calling him "Tarzan."

An old Native American's estimate of a minister noted for loud, but useless, preaching: "Big wind, great thunder, but no rain."

L.H., AZ

In a pastor's dreams:
People saying, "Hey! It's my turn to sit in the front pew!"

My twelve-year-old daughter and I always pray together before she goes to bed. On one recent evening I left her room grinning. As part of her petitions she had prayed, "And help Daddy get a raise soon—that's 'soon' in people time, God, not in your time."

E.N., IL

As my young grandson and I were driving home from our Lutheran church service, we passed another church which was located by a busy pedestrian crosswalk. There was a warning sign on the corner that he read slowly to me: "Watch out for Presbyterians."

P.B., NE

A young pastor was driving home from church with his four-year-old son. The boy noticed a man walking his beautiful Dalmatian dog and said with excitement, "Look, Dad! A damnation!"

E.P., NE

Before the church collection, a man read from the Scriptures, "Do you have any idea what I have done for all of you?" A little kid hollered, "Yeah!"

A.K., WA

In the middle of the sermon one little kid turned to another and said, "We have to be quiet or we'll get in trouble with the hushers."

The primary Bible history class was reviewing the lesson on creation. It was already established that on the sixth day God created Adam and Eve. The teacher then asked, "How did God create both Adam and Eve?" A first grader confidently and sincerely answered, "Naked!"

L.B., NE

Teacher: "Who wrote the Psalms?"
Smart-alec kid: "Psalmbody!"

K.P., NE

One Sunday in church I was sitting behind two families, each with a three-year-old—one a girl, one a boy. The boy was playing quietly, and when the little girl started talking loudly, he scolded her, saying, "SHHH! We're in church. Besides, there are people sleeping here!" (And—of course—the boy was the pastor's kid.)

L.P., KS

At church camp this summer, several young people were baptized. Walking back to the cabins one evening, I overheard one seven-year-old girl say that she wanted to be baptized, too. Her counselor remarked that this was wonderful, but that she was probably too young to completely understand about being baptized. The girl responded, "Oh, yes, I do! All you have to do is say 'yes, yes, yes' to all the questions, hold your nose, and don't breathe when they put you under the water."

B.J.H., KS

During a lesson on sharing, the Sunday school teacher pinched a piece of cookie off and gave it to a little kid. The next in line, a husky boy, said, "I'm a lot bigger so I'll need a bigger piece."

K.P., NE

Ever heard the Easter song about "Gravy Rose"?

A.B., NJ

Or how about the stirring hymn that begins, "Lead on, O kinky turtle"?

Books of the Old Testament: "Job, Psalms, Proverbs . . . Enthusiastics."

"Teachable moments" can sometimes backfire. One of our denominational executives, speaking in church recently, shared the story of how he decided to use the "WWJD" ("What Would Jesus

Do?") craze among youth to his parental advantage. Noticing the sorry state of his son's room, he asked the youngster, "What would Jesus do about cleaning his room?"

"Oh," came the confident response, "he'd just pray and *zap!* everything would be cleaned up."

In another "what Jesus *wouldn't* do" situation, I was lecturing my daughter about not working on a school project she had known about for weeks until the night before it was due. Hoping she would learn from the consequences, I said, "You'll have to tell the teacher you didn't finish it, and he'll take it off your grade."

"I could lie and say I left it on the kitchen counter," she suggested hopefully.

I pointed to her bracelet. "See what that says? Jesus would never lie. Jesus is Truth itself. So what *would* Jesus do here?"

"Jesus would never have gotten himself into this mess in the first place," she retorted.

Try arguing with that kind of logic.

E.N., IL

While teaching my preschool class about guilt and what it means to do bad things, I asked one child if she felt bad after she disobeyed her mommy. She answered, "No, but it makes my mommy feel bad."

C.W., NC

As I showed my first grade class a picture of Jesus holding up his hands and preaching to his disciples, I asked them what they thought he was saying. One child said, "He's telling them to be good." Another said, "To not be naughty."

The third child had a different take. She said, "He's telling them that he'll be back next Sunday."

E.W., AZ

I was teaching a kindergarten class a lesson about Jesus dying on the cross, and I asked, "Who knows what Jesus said before he died?"

No one said anything for the longest time, until one fellow raised his hand and declared, "Jesus said, 'Good luck, everybody.'"

K.T., OK

Every child in class was supposed to use the word "heaven" in a sentence.

The first kid said, "When I die I hope to go to heaven."

The second kid said, "Heaven is where God lives."

The third kid said, "My mom is heaven another headache."

F.J., FL

One kid was happy that she belonged to her church, because "you don't have to go through a percolator to get to heaven like Catholics do."

G.H., AR

My six-year-old daughter was asked what church she attended. She thought and said, "I can't remember exactly, but it's one of the Lutheran churches." Later she exclaimed, "I remember now! It's the German Shepherd Lutheran Church!"

E.J., OK

The preschool class lesson was about the miracle of Jesus feeding the five thousand with five loaves and two fish. The teacher asked, "How do you think Jesus could feed so many people with so little food?"

One child answered, "My mommy makes 'Clean the Refrigerator Soup' with just a little bit of food; maybe that's what he did."

C.B., MN

A five-year-old's explanation of creation: "Then God put Adam to sleep and took out a wishbone to make the lady."

C.A., KS

A father's annoying joke of poking his yawning kid's tongue, abruptly ended in the middle of a church service after his finger went too far, the kid gagged, and then threw up all over the floor.

L.A., NC

In the children's Christmas play, Joseph asked the innkeeper if they had any room. The innkeeper said, "No, we have no room." He forgot his next line but improvised by saying, ". . . but why don't you come on in and have a drink?"

S.F., AR

When my niece, Janet, and nephew, Jim, were preschoolers, the Sunday-school class was to sing a couple of children's carols at the church's Christmas program. They practiced in their classroom and at the front of the church (minus an audience, of course) for weeks. Finally the big night arrived, and every child was scrubbed, combed, and festively clothed. The teachers herded the children to the front of the church and lined them up. The pianist began playing "Away in a Manger." Jim and Janet took one look at the large congregation—and both froze. Upon returning home after the program, we walked into the kitchen and Jim let out a giant sigh. "Boy!" he declared. "It sure is a lot harder singing than talking!"

I.T., NE

It was Christmas Eve in rural upstate New York. The children were prepared to reenact the Nativity scene one more time. The littlest ones had been included as well, with short, simple lines such as "angels singing," "crowds rejoicing," etc. Nathan's turn came. Dorothy stood in front of the children ready to prompt them when trouble came. Nathan mumbled something. Dorothy shook her head and stage-whispered his lines to him. He mumbled again. She repeated the words. With a frown,

Nathan drew a deep breath and shouted, "Bells are ringing, I TOLD YOU!!!"

M.J.K., IA

In a small-town church in western Kentucky, I was giving my usual children's message. It was around Christmastime and we were discussing the colors that often symbolize the holiday. Trying to bring the point home to them, I asked, "When you ride through town, what do you see that's red and green?" After pondering awhile and coming up with everything but the correct response, one child piped up, "Tractors!"

M.J.K., IA

Our "Joseph" in the Christmas pageant walked impressively down the aisle, leading Mary and the donkey. Suddenly Joseph saw a man sitting at the end of a pew and used his staff to soundly bonk this man on the head. Then he continued down the aisle. After the service, when his horrified mother asked why on earth he had struck this gentleman, Joseph replied, "He was making funny faces at me."

It was a Christmas service and there was a Nativity scene by the altar. The priest asked all the little children to come up to the front to see it. He asked the question, "What should be done to keep the baby Jesus warm?" One child said to put him in a blanket, another said to put straw around the manger, but the third child responded, "Shut the door!"

D.F., NE

When asked if he had a real Christmas tree or a fake one, a child answered, "We have a real one, like the Bible says."

J.S., OH

Because she thought God was probably bored with hearing her same old prayers every night, one little girl decided to tell him the story of the baby Jesus and the manger, just in case he hadn't heard it before.

A little boy came up to the preacher and said, "Your sermons are boring and confusing." Sure made my day.

H.M., NE

I was sitting in the front row with my outspoken three-year-old listening to a missionary speak on the Lord's work in Africa. The missionary apologized for his speech, which was somewhat mumbled because of a case of shingles he had on his face. My youngster asked, "Why that man talk funny?" I told him to shush and I'd tell him after church. "But, Mom, he talks so funny, how come?" On and on and on he went, until he said loudly, "Mom, he says ba, bla, ba, bla, ba, bla." The missionary heard this and stared at me until I shrank. I've never been so embarrassed in my life.

J.G., NE

Every time this elderly man would lead us in prayer, it seemed his pleas would get longer and longer. One Sunday as he prayed, my three-year-old niece got impatient and hollered loudly, "Amen!"

The whole congregation started laughing and the man concluded his prayer quickly.

A.T., NE

It was my turn to recite the memory verse for the pastor. I said, "He that heareth me, heareth you, and . . . uh—uh—" I couldn't remember the rest, so I said, "He that heareth you, heareth me." The pastor whispered to me, "Despiseth."

"Oh, yeah," I said, relieved. "He that despiseth me, despiseth you."

L.U., NE

Years ago my young son went to the front of the church to take part in the children's lesson. The topic was praising God through song, and the lesson leader mentioned a few of his favorite hymns. He then asked the children if they had any favorites. My son said, "How about the one that starts 'From the land of sky-blue waters'?" This was the jingle from a beer commercial.

During the Communion service, a four-year-old boy was giving his mom trouble about not letting him have any of the "cracker" that was being passed around. He said, "OK, but when the Kool-Aid man comes by, I want some!"

M.D., ID

The teacher was talking to her preschool class about how Jesus will take your sins away. My four-year-old nephew asked, "When will Jesus give them back?"

"He never does," she said.

"That's not very nice, to take something and not give it back," my nephew declared.

S.K., NE

A young newcomer to a Catholic church noticed people were kneeling before they sat down and asked what they were doing. The friend told her they were "genuflecting." The youngster said, "Why don't they just call it squatting?"

M.A., NE

While preaching, a sermon the pastor noticed people in the last rows looking down at the floor. He didn't think much about it until the "wave" started advancing toward the front, with each successive row of people peering down. Finally, out from under the first pew emerged his own kid—his one-year-old son, who somehow had escaped his mom's grasp and crawled under all the pews on his way to the front.

J.S., NE

I'm a nurse in a hospital surgical wing. One day a six-year-old boy was in the recovery room. Since he was still asleep, I went back out to the nurses' station and the boy's mom stepped out to grab a cup of coffee. He must have rolled around a bit in his bed, inadvertently pressing the "call" button for the nurses' station on his intercom control. Out at the nurses' station, I responded through the intercom, "Yes, Bobby?"

There was no answer, so I tried again: "Yes, Bobby?" Still no answer.

Becoming just a bit concerned, I said, "Bobby, are you there?" Then came the timid reply: "Yes . . . God."

J.D., NE

A friend of mine tells of a little girl who attended church with her mother and suddenly began to feel ill.

"Mama," she said, "I have to go throw up."

"Hurry around to the little garden in back of the church," her mom said.

Presently the girl returned and her mother asked, "Were you there and back already?"

"Oh, I didn't have to go way out there," replied the tot. "I saw a box in the back of the church which said, 'For the Sick.'"

D.R., NE

As a little kid tried to toss his quarter in the collection plate, it missed and fell to the floor, making quite a ruckus.

Another kid close by said loudly, "Air ball!"

B.A., NE

As an usher passing the collection plate one Sunday, I waited while a couple who had given their daughter a dime struggled to get her to let go of it. As they pried it from her fingers, she angrily yelled, "I don't see why I have to pay anything, I didn't want to come here anyway!"

C.H., NE

Years ago my three-year-old cousin was standing on the pew beside me holding his own hymnal when he leaned over and asked, "What channel are we on?"

R.B., VT

Noticing so many restaurants and stores open on Sunday, my husband and I started reminiscing about when we were kids and Sundays were special because nobody worked. My six-year-old looked puzzled and asked, "I wonder if working on Sunday makes God mad?"

D.O., KS

I was in a health-food store when a fellow with long hair, beard, and white robe came in to do some shopping. I could feel my toddler staring at this man, but felt there was nothing I could do about it. All of a sudden the ice broke when my seven-year-old said to her little sister, "No, Regan, it's not God!"

A.R., NE

A minister was trying to explain the Lord's Supper to a group of children. He compared it to having a kind of party. Hoping for a response like "celebrate," he asked the group, "What do people do at your house when there's a party?" One kid said, "Go crazy!"

J.H., NE

When my boys were little, if one of our goldfish died, we would have a little funeral, say the Lord's Prayer, and flush the fish down the toilet. As my boys grew up and had their own families, they carried on the same tradition.

While attending a funeral with my granddaughter, who was barely old enough to talk, she said—you guessed it—"Are we gonna flush her?"

M.G., NE

Our family attended a funeral where the remains were cremated, put in an urn, wrapped, and presented to the family. My four-year-old niece turned to me and said, "Who gets to open the present?"

P.W., NE

We were in a church service where the preacher asked for a moment of silence so we could reflect on our blessings. When all was quiet and everyone was in silent meditation, some kid whistled "Shave and a Haircut, Two Bits."

M.P., OK

When my son was about six, he and I discussed the Resurrection and the meaning of Easter. I explained things the best I could to a lad of his under-standing, and he said, "Now I've heard everything."

W.K., WA

A new kid joined the second grade at a Catholic school. On the second day, he raised his hand and signaled Number One. Sister Christine said, "Mark, you may leave the room." Mark left but was soon back saying, "I can't find it, Sister!"

Sister Christine asked Bernard to go with Mark and help him find it. He and Mark left the room and in five minutes returned and took their seats. Mark was grinning from ear to ear. "We found it, Sister, I had my pants on backwards!"

C.T., SD

A little boy was being disruptive during Mass. In desperation his mother gave him her rosary to play with. Suddenly he started whirling it over his head and hollered, "Hang on, Jesus, you're goin' for a ride!"

K.A., NE

I was behind the stage curtain of our Fellowship hall. I was aware of several kids on the stage steps, but they didn't know I could hear their conversation. One boy, about five, told another of the same age, "Randy thinks you're a nerd!" That phrase caught my attention, and I assumed I would be in the midst of breaking up a quarrel within minutes. However, the statement that followed caused a deafening silence: "What kind of nerd?"

If we each could but measure our responses with such wisdom!

J.K., KS

Children's responses:

Noah's wife was called Joan of Ark.

The epistles are the wives of the apostles.

The Fourth Commandment is: Humor thy father and mother.

Lot's wife was a pillar of salt by day, and a ball of fire by night.

The tower of Babel is where Solomon kept his wives.

When Mary heard she was to be the mother of Jesus, she went off and sang the Magna Carta.

Holy Acrimony is another name for marriage.

The Eighth Commandment is: Thou shalt not witness thy bare neighbor.

Christians have only one wife. They call it monotony.

Paraffin is next in order to seraphin.

Adam and Eve had twins: Cain and Mable.

B.M., IN

I heard of a very strict Mennonite pastor who took his five-year-old son out of church for discipline. The boy thought he was being treated unfairly. Later that day, the pastor took his son to a men's business meeting and made him sit in the corner until the meeting was over.

At this time the boy got his revenge. He said to the group, "My dad will probably deny this, but he smokes sometimes!"

P.J., CA

On Lutheran confirmation day, the pastor asked the question, "Who started the church?" One excited boy eagerly waved his hand, much to his mother's pride, and when called on said, "MARTIN LUTHER KING!"

N.C., NE

The kid had forgotten that he was supposed to recite the Twenty-third Psalm that night at church. All Sunday afternoon he crammed it into his head. He was so preoccupied with the verses that when the phone rang, he answered it, "The Lord is my shepherd."

A.K., WA

While reciting the Hail Mary, my three-year-old friend declared, "Messed up is the fruit in your room" instead of "Blessed is the fruit of your womb."

J.J., NY

The fourth-grade Sunday-school class was working with acronyms for Lent. Such ideas as "Let's Eliminate Negative Thinking" were suggested, but one boy proposed "The Lord Eats Noodles Today."

(Must be Friday.)

J.J., NY

During a solemn ceremony, as the altar boys lit candles, our three-year-old sang out, "Happy birthday to you!"

S.K., NE

A kid says, "If we were made out of the dust of the earth, why don't we turn to mud when we get rained on?"

K.P., NE

During a "Pew Packers" session, where the small children answer Bible questions, the teacher asked a little boy named Seth who the first three sons of Adam and Eve were. He could only think of Cain and Abel until the teacher said, "The third one has your name." The boy said, "Cain, Abel, and Seth!"

When the teacher asked the little girl next to him to recite them, she said, "Cain, Abel, and Janie!"

B.J.H., KS

A preschool member of my Sunday school class was not very impressed with the story of Martha anointing Jesus' feet with perfume. He exclaimed, "We put perfume here" (pointing to his armpit), "not on our feet!"

On the way home from Sunday school, his father asked him what he had learned that day. He responded that the story had been about some woman putting deodorant on Jesus. His father had some questions for me the next Sunday.

J.D., NE

During the middle of the church service I took my eyes off my toddler son for just a minute, and by the time I turned back to him, he had taken off his dirty diaper and was standing at the end of the pew about to leave.

V.Y., NE

This kid almost had it right when he said, "I believe in Jesus Christ, the only forgotten Son of God."

J.S., AR

Talk about shades of meaning: In our church we are taught that when we are baptized we become "new creatures in Christ." This is one youngster's interpretation of that statement: "Baptism makes us new animals for God."

K.I., MN

One little fellow was overheard singing, "Microwave the boat ashore, alleluia."

R.D., MN

At one Lutheran church, the question was asked of the first grade class, "Can anyone name the four Gospels?"

During the service I took my eyes off my toddler for just a minute . . .

One boy answered, "Matthew, Mark, Luther, and John."

C.K., MI

I had invited a substitute lay preacher to fill in for me. She asked people in the congregation to share their favorite Bible verses. After this was finished she asked, "What do all these Bible verses have in common?" One of the youngsters piped up, "All the people who wrote them are dead."

M.J.K., IA

I showed my class a picture of Jesus and one of the kids asked why he wasn't smiling. A less-than-enthusiastic child remarked, "Because he had to go to church again."

E.K., TN

As we parked our car in the church parking lot, I saw the new vicar going into the church. I asked my six-year-old daughter if she knew who that man was. She answered, "Yes, that's the man that wants to be a pastor when he grows up."

L.N., SD

The pastor's first sentence of his sermon was "Lo, I am with you always."

My restless daughter said, "Oh, no. We're going to be here a long time!"

B.T., AR

A young boy was reciting the books of the Old Testament: "Amos, Obadiah . . ." He couldn't remember any more so the teacher gave him a hint: "He was swallowed by a whale."

The boy brightened. "Oh yeah!" he exclaimed. "Pinocchio!"

B.S., NE

My young son was watching the people in our congregation go up to the front for Communion. He asked me why they were doing this and what Communion means. I explained to him that this was a very special way of remembering that Jesus had suffered for us all by being nailed to the cross and dying for our sins. This made him look very sober, and then he asked earnestly, "Well, where were the police?"

P.B., NE

I am a lifestyle writer for the *Chattanooga Free Press* newspaper. Once I was interviewing kindergartners for their views on the Crucifixion. The most interesting interpretation I heard had to do with Jesus' being hung "on the Red Cross" before being put in a "sealed tube." The same group identified "mayonnaise" as their favorite hymn. It sounded a lot like "Amazing Grace" when they sang it for me.

J.G., TN

The church of my childhood has a very large and formal Georgian-style sanctuary, with a long, narrow chancel area. At the very back of the chancel was a white altar. When I was a little kid I never saw anyone go up to the altar except the pastors, so I imagined it was a sort of Protestant Holy of Holies, a place where God dwelt, or maintained a vacation home when things got too hectic in heaven. At the very least, I thought that the altar housed objects too sacred ever to be seen, something like saintly relics in medieval cathedrals.

Twenty or so years later I happened to be helping out with something at church one weekday and wandered into the sanctuary. Imagine my shock when I saw the grizzled old sexton calmly walk up to the altar, unlock the front panel, open it and take out a mop and bucket. My Holy of Holies was actually a broom closet!

E.N., IL

Let Us Gather for Prayer and Medication:
Real Stuff People Have Typed Wrong

Church bulletin: "ORDER OR WORSHIP."

Sermon: "Biting Off More Than You Can Chew."
Communion Hymn: "Let Us Break Bread Together."

"In order that a pastor of this congregation may be devoted to the duties of the office, an adequate salary shall be provided, pain in semimonthly or monthly installments."

A church ran a "pastor wanted" classified advertisement in the denominatinal magazine. The ad read, "Starts August 6. Send resumé by June 1. Include wife, transcripts, and references."

 O.Y., OK

One church sent out a notice of its congregational meeting "to decide questions concerning the furnace and the pastoral call."

"Sermon title: 'The Devil Speaks.' Pastor Bill will be giving the sermon."

From the minutes of a church council meeting: "The pulpit loudspeaker sys-

"Order or Worship"

tem was discussed; there have been complaints of being able to hear the sermon."

"Come and celebrate! Pastor Steve will present his last sermon on Sunday."

Two messages on a church signboard:
PASTOR BOB IS ON VACATION.
PRAISE THE LORD!

Two more messages on a signboard:
SUNDAY MORNING SERMON: "JESUS WALKING ON WATER."
SUNDAY EVENING SERMON: "LOOKING FOR JESUS."

Here he is:
"Please note in your church directory the Lord's new address (the phone number will remain the same)." The Lord family had bought a new house.

This notice was left on the door for the Hispanic custodian of a California church: "Dear Jesus—Please buff the floor and lock up when you leave."

"Tickets for the drawing can be purchased as you pass out after services."

"Each Wednesday during Advent, the congregation will gather for prayer, medication, and preparation."

"Don't let worry kill you off. Let the church help."

"Remember in prayer the many who are sick of our church and community."

"Thank you for your sympathy and the lovely pot plant."

"The outreach committee has enlisted twenty-five volunteers to make calls on people who are not afflicted with any church."

As the coffin was lifted and carried to the altar, more than three thousand mourners sang the hymn, "O God, Our Health and Age Has Past."

Gives new meaning to the phrase "She was a pillar of our church": "Lunch will be served following the burial in the church basement."

And you think you've got problems:
"A most sincere thank-you to everyone for all the cards, prayers, and words of encouragement during my illness and death."

"We offer prayers of thanksgiving on behalf of Jeremy W., who has been experiencing health problems. He has undergone a recent brain scan, and they didn't find anything."

"Miss Mable Johnson will be entering the hospital this week for testes."

"John Simpson died early Tuesday. The congregation joins in wishing him a speedy recovery."

"Helen White has been taken seriously. She is in Memorial Hospital."

In my hometown newspaper one day, the obituaries ran in column one and the funeral notices were in column four on the same page. I found it amusing that sandwiched between these somber columns the newspaper had run a huge ad stating "*News-Times*—the newspaper that wakes up the city!"

When the church becomes a business . . .
Organ prelude: "Jesus, Priceless Treasurer."

Next hymn: "Jesus Paid It All $156" (instead of #156).

Hymn #67: "Away in a Manager."

Offertory: "Steal Away."

Closing prayer: "May we workshop you in spirit and truth."

"Council Report—Due to the length of the Parish Council meeting, very little business was conducted."
(I've sat through some of those.)

"The Spring Council Retreat will be hell May 10 and 11."

"The correspondence committee will assist with the mailing of the newsletter and stapling of the Annual Report to congregational members."

"There will be a congregational meeting after the worship service to approve next year's budget. Please plan not to attend."

"Sunday we will hold a service at which we will also install our new and old leadership and deceive new members."

"Jane Elliot, president, opened the meeting with a poem. The Lord's Prayer was then read and approved."

One student may have said more than she meant when she wrote about the Apostles' Creed, that she believed in "one holy chaotic church."

And one boy spoke of baptism by saying, "Unlike the Baptists who believe in total erosion, we Lutherans believe . . ."

So it comes as no surprise that . . .
"There will not be a Week of Prayer for United Service next Sunday, due to schedule conflicts for five of the six congregations involved."

"Ninety percent of ELCA congregations have one or fewer families."

"Adult dinner menu: Road beef, potatoes, and gravy."

(Saw it on the way to church.)

"Everyone helping with the used clothing roundup will be heaving a potluck."

"Before the lecture he will be discussing his personal faith struggle in suffering at a potluck dinner."

"In conjunction with the annual meeting, a lunch persisting of spaghetti and meatballs will be served."

(Leftovers again!)

"The Junior Ladies' Guild will have a benefit luncheon on Saturday. They will be serving the same wonderful meal they served last year."

No comment . . .
From 1 Corinthians 13, as typed in a bulletin: "Lover never faileth."

"Cheerfulness promotes health and immorality."

A church secretary wrote that she thankfully caught this error before the bulletin was printed: "Pastor John will deliver the Advent massage."

"Gifts and Memorials: $400 for Elevator Fun given by Helen."

The special music was listed as "Communion Motel" (instead of "motet").

"Let goods and kindred go, thy moral life also . . ."
(We don't think this is exactly what Luther had in mind.)

"Michael and Deborah were married on October 24 in the church. So ends a friendship that began in school days."

"There will be a baby shower for Rachel Hanson, expecting twins today, Nov. 2, from 2-4."

Muscular Christianity: "Following the meeting they will go out and pick up their section of Hwy. 34."

"Tom Clark and Bill Schmidt will be moving the church lawn this week."

"The Johnson family will be attending the funeral of Susie's former husband, who died in Detroit, Mich., tomorrow."

"Next Sunday's Forum will deal with the subject of cremation. The guest speaker will be Mike Ashburn."

"Please greet the newest embers in Fellowship Hall."

"Sermon: 'How to Burn without Burning Out.' Pastor Wick."

The radio hostess was talking about the importance of Christian music in our lives. She said, "Christian music has always been part of our Christian heresy."

Someone had called the bakery to order a cake inscribed, "Happy Birthday, Pastor Bock." As the chaplain entered the lounge, he was startled to see the message on the frosting: "Happy Birthday, Pass the Buck."

"Many items have been left in the church during the past several weeks, including hates, gloves, umbrellas, and coats."

"George Butler's name was intentionally omitted from the list of Sunday school teachers."

Male and female he created them . . .
Meeting topic: "Women's rule in the church."

"As soon as the weather clears, the men will have a goof outing."

"Fellowship hour with display of guilts by women of Grace Church."

"The extension office will present a program on premenstrual syndrome and how it affects women at St. Matthew Lutheran Church."

"The men not only helped set up, but cooked the children and cleaned up after!"

Our church newsletter advertised a men's fishing retreat weekend complete with cabins, boatslips, lake, and lodge for $25 a reservation. The date for the weekend was listed as "March 30–June 1."

(Talk about your male bonding. . . .)

"Hymn #234: Wise Up, O Men of God."

"If you received a Christmas fruit basket from Augustana, if possible, please return it to the church by next November."

"The Christmas decorating party for church starts Sunday at 2 P.M. Bring your saws to cut trees and willing hands."

"The Tired Sunday in Advent."
(Yep, the Christmas rush will do that to you.)

"Christmas luncheon at the Quality Inn. Lunch at 12:30. Bring an unwrapped gift or man or lady."

"The Salvation Army would appreciate receiving canned or boxed groceries, good used sweaters and good used boys for their Christmas assistance program."

"Lent provides addictional opportunities for worship and prayer."

Preparation for Lent included the traditional Shrove Tuesday supper. In the monthly church calendar the invitation read, "Shove Dinner with Service."

The Palm Sunday bulletin read, "The palm branches will be collected as you leave to be burned."

"Holy Saturday—Easter Vigil—7:30 P.M." "Easier Festival Service—10:30 A.M."

Our church's Easter breakfast was listed as "No Resurrection Necessary" to be admitted.

Huh?

"Easter Sunrise Service, Sunday, 6 P.M."

"Midnight Mass will begin at 10 P.M."

"Confirmation classes will be held the second and fourth Sundays of each week."

"Spend one Sunday a week at your nearest church."

"The men's fellowship breakfast will meet Tuesday at 12 sharp."

"We will be having only one service this summer beginning at 9 A.M. June 5, continuing through Sept. 15."

For the coffee hour, the announcement read, "The Heinz family is furnishing threats this morning."

"Our picture gallery is being updated by Gary. Please cooperate when he approaches you to be shot."

"Anyone not at the church parking lot by noon will be executed."

"Children will be given sermon-related bulleting by the ushers for use during the worship service."

Not only that, but . . . "Ushers will eat latecomers at these points."

"The concert held in the Fellowship Hall was a great success. Special thanks are due to the minister's daughter, who labored the whole evening at the piano, which as usual fell upon her."

"Henrietta Turner will offer a rare vocal threat as she presents a selection of eighteenth-century hymns."

"This evening's songs will be taken from the Scared Collection Hymnal."

"*Please cooperate as you are approached to be shot for our photo gallery.*"

Sing along with . . .
"Table My life, and Let It Be"

"When We Meet in Tweet Communion"

"Prince of Peach, Control My Will"

"To Go Be the Glory"

"Jesus Lies, and So Shall I"
(You will. He won't.)

"The 'Over 60s' choir will be disbanded for the summer with the thanks of the entire church."

A congregation of Swedish heritage listed the hymn, "Amazing Grace, How Swede the Sound."

"A worm welcome to Kathy, our guest organist."

The prelude for June 21 was listed as *Pop and Circumstance*. Appropriately, that Sunday was Father's Day.

During the dedication of the new public-address .system, one of the congregational responses in the bulletin read, "God bless our sound reproduction facilities!"

"Musician Wanted: Must be able to play piano in Spanish."

"7:20 A.M. Jr. Choir's trip to Noah's Ark. Rain date is June 27."

"Eight new black choir robes are currently needed, due to the addition of several new members and to the deterioration of some older ones."

"We have a wonderful time at Wednesday night service, so why come."

A near-universal sentiment:
"Let me be thin forever."

"He that believes in him shall have ever-laughing life."

And All God's People Blurted . . .
Miscellaneous Stories and Silliness

One lady turned to me after church and said, "Your baby is two of my favorite kinds—asleep and somebody else's."

S.C., NE

A mother's prayer for her child: "Thank God he's in bed."

R.P., IL

Martha, the custodian at our church, is a real tyrant. Everyone fears her wrath, including our pastor. No one dares to track in dirt, rearrange the hymnals, or do anything else without securing her approval. One day my daughter was telling me what she wanted to be when she grew up. "I want to be a pastor, Mom," she said. I regretfully told her that our church doesn't allow female pastors. She then decided she would be an elder. "Nope, no female elders allowed either," I said.

She was silent and thoughtful for a minute, then brightened and exclaimed, "Okay, then I'll be a custodian like Martha. She runs the church anyway."

When I lived in northwestern Wisconsin, in red clay country, it had rained for days on end. Early one Sunday morning the pastor called to ask me to pick up a couple of girls for Sunday school. They usually rode with a couple who lived near them, but the couple was out of town that day. The girls lived off the gravel road a couple of hundred yards. My car slipped and slid all the way through the mud of the driveway, through the rain that continued to pour, up to their front door. Rather than just honk the horn, I got out of the car and sloshed to their front porch. Without opening the door, the older girl shouted to me through a window, "Go around to the back!" Her younger sister's voice was clearly heard, "Don't he know nothin'? Everybody goes to the back."

So I went back to the car, got in, and drove around to the back. I parked, got out again, and squished to the back door. This time the door was opened and the older girl told me, with an utterly deadpan expression, "We ain't goin' today." After more than thirteen years in the military, I was able to handle it with a straight face.

R.A., AZ

After several weeks of extremely hot summer weather, the sign in the church-yard read, "And You Think THIS Is Hot!"

Another churchyard sign: "We're going to heaven someday. If you need a ride, give us a call."

Bumper sticker: "I'm laying my treasures up in heaven . . . just look at my car."

Another bumper sticker: "Trust in God—She will provide."

Sign on the door of a Hong Kong dentist: "Teeth extracted by latest methodists."

A sign in front of a church under construction read, "Danger, Men Working Above." I thought to myself, *Isn't that the truth, when men try to take the place of God?*
    S.C., NE

Toward the end of the church service, our song director reported that last Sunday's special collection had raised only half the money needed for our new hymnals. He said the church couldn't order them until the full amount was raised, so there was to be another special collection today and each following Sunday until the money was in hand. "So," he concluded, "you can either dig deep today or pull the scab off slowly—it doesn't matter. We will raise the money sooner or later."
    (I guess that's one way of saying it.)
        C.R., NE

Someone told me that an Episcopalian was a Catholic who had flunked Latin.

One lady asked if a turkey that had been in her freezer for twenty-three years would be safe to eat. The answer was, "Yes, if it has never been thawed, but the quality would not be good."

The lady responded, "That's what I thought. I'll give it to the church."

(Yes, and the church also wants all those canned goods that have sat around in your pantry for years because no one in your family can stand to eat them.)

K.A., NE

During my Catholic wedding ceremony, my husband-to-be and I each read biblical passages. The text my husband read (I think it came from 1 or 2 Corinthians) included a reference to having chosen a bride "after zealous investigation." My husband chose me, however, after "zealous indigestion."

J.G., TN

One Sunday the church bulletin was typed on pretty pink paper. The pastor announced that he had done this on purpose to remind everyone that Valentine's Day was coming. One man in the congregation muttered that the pink paper reminded him of Pepto Bismol.

A.S., NE

If God didn't mean for me to go fishing on Sunday morning, he wouldn't have made them bite so good at that time.

P.R., AR

I sell handmade Christmas ornaments at craft shows. One day an elderly nun bought two children's ornaments from me. I asked her, "Are these for your grandchildren?" Oops.

L.N., NE

On the way out of a prison service, one well-meaning church lady said, "Come and visit us any time," as if they could.

J.C., NE

We were singing "All Hail the Power of Jesus' Name" when I overheard the man behind me sing, "Let angels prostate fall."

R.M., LA

Out of respect for a dear, hundred-year-old lady, the congregation sang "Happy Birthday" to her. After everyone applauded, the song director said that we were dismissed. He stopped, looked stupid, and asked one of the elders if it was scriptural to close a service with the singing of "Happy Birthday." Since half the people were already in the aisles, he said it was okay this time.

G.D., MT

Whoever was supposed to say the closing prayer wasn't around to do it, so eventually two different men got up from different sides of the building to fill in. They unexpectedly met on the stage, and then each decided to let the other guy say the prayer, and then both turned to go back to their seats. Neither man knew what to do until the preacher finally pointed his finger at one of them.

A.Z., CA

A few years ago I was minister of music in a Baptist church in Stockton, California. One day when the pastor was out, the fire marshal, along with a couple of firefighters, came by the church to do a fire safety inspection. At the conclusion of the inspection they gave me a verbal report. One of the firemen, making reference to the baptistry, said, in all sincerity, "Oh, by the way, you got some crickets in your hot tub."

R.W., TN

While lingering in front of the Catholic church, my cousin was having one last cigarette before attending his first mass. He had never been to church, but I had finally convinced him to go with me.

As services started, I led the way inside the foyer, only to turn around and see my cousin douse his cigarette in the holy water receptacle. He said he didn't know whether to throw it away outside or if there was an ashtray inside. When he saw the water, he didn't know any better but thought it very convenient for the church to put one of those things there.

A.S., NE

My mom was tired of my dad serving on time-consuming church boards and holding various offices. When he told her he was thinking about becoming an elder (for about the third time in ten years), she put her foot down. "If you decide to become an elder again," she threatened, "I'll leave you, and you'll be automatically disqualified!"

K.A., NE

My aunt and uncle arrived late at the family reunion. They'd had a special service at church, followed by two guest speakers. My uncle commented that the speakers were interesting, but the morning had certainly gone on too long. "After all," he said mischievously, "the mind can only absorb as long as the rear can endure."

C.B., NE

While I was listening to a radio broadcast of a church service, the station went off the air. About a minute or two later it came back on and the radio announcer said, "Due to circumstances beyond our control, we will now return you to the worship service."

My first two years of college were spent at a local Christian school. One of the requirements was that you take a Bible class every semester. I was still living at home and regularly attended church, where my dad was the minister. I thought I would kill two birds with one stone by doing my college Bible assignments during church. This worked pretty well until one Sunday afternoon, when Dad asked me what I had been doing during the service, since he had noticed my head was bowed throughout the sermon. I told him, and he thought a moment, then said, "Well, don't you think you should be listening to the sermon?"

I'll bet that was the only time since Adam met Eve that someone got into trouble for studying the Bible in church.

B.P., TX

My preacher told a hilarious story one Sunday about how we do stupid things sometimes and end up paying the price. He compared it to something he did as a child when he and his buddies went out to an empty grain bin. He looked in the doorway and noticed dozens of pigeons roosting inside. He told his friends to watch the pigeons fly when he scared them. He climbed inside the bin and screamed at the top of his lungs, causing a flurry of pigeon activity. He paused in his sermon for a moment and said, "Do you have any idea what a hundred pigeons do when they're scared?"

K.A., NE

Things Pondered during Dry Sermons

Some people sow their oats on Saturday night and pray for crop failure Sunday morning.

If loud children bother you in church, odds are you are sitting in the back.

Instead of buying the boy a Bible, they told him his name was Gideon and took one from a motel.

What exactly can a mortuary screw up?

Why don't people tear out their offering checks BEFORE church, instead of making so much noise IN church?

Is purgatory the hundred feet between the "Leaving Nebraska" sign and the "Entering Kansas" sign?

Funny how laborious it can be to read a chapter in the Bible, but how easy it is to read a three-hundred page novel.

It is usually the rich who say to the poor, "Be of good cheer."

Some say, "Get thee behind me, Satan," then put him in their hip pocket.

The best place to criticize your neighbor is in front of your own mirror.

Happiness is waking up thinking you have to go to work, then remembering it's Sunday.

K.A., NE

I left the door open at the local cafe, and one crony said, "Were you born in a barn?" I said, "Yes, me and Jesus."

R.M., TN

I was in a Bible class with a self-proclaimed biblical genius. He got caught not knowing as much as he let on. His comeback: "I know all about that, but I've been sworn to secrecy."

W.T., ND

One man's excuse for never shoveling the snow: "The Lord giveth, the Lord taketh away."

E.B., NE

At the end of a marriage counseling session, the wife was putting on her coat and she asked her husband if it made her look fat. He said, "No, but your rear end does." I asked her to wait in the car while I had another talk with her husband.

J.L., NE

Biblical reason for the husband to help around the kitchen: Second Kings 21:13,

"I will wipe Jerusalem as a man wipeth a dish, wiping it and turning it upside down."

P.L., OK

After singing the closing hymn, a visitor in front of me turned and said on his way out, "Don't give up your day job."

R.S., NY

A friend of mine went into the confessional, and instead of saying the customary "Bless me, Father, for I have sinned," she absent-mindedly began reciting the common table prayer, "Come, Lord Jesus, be our guest. . . ." Fortu-

After singing the closing hymn, another worshiper turned to me and said, "Don't give up your day job."

nately, the priest had a terrific sense of humor, because he interrupted her and chuckled, "What'd you do, bring your lunch?"

L.M., NE

At a large fish fry, a brother in Christ asked, "How long have you been preaching?" When I told him, my younger brother, whom I had been trying to convert for some time, said, "Huh! He's been preaching a long longer than that—he's just getting paid for it now."

M.G., KS

My arthritis doctor told me he didn't want me on my knees unless I heard the Lord was coming.

M.J., SC

As I was driving down the highway, I passed "Anderson Cemetery." I thought, *Who would want a cemetery named after them? Let's see . . . Alley Cemetery. . . . Nope, doesn't do a thing for me.*

K.A, NE

As I was listening to our pastor speak on the subject of adultery, a helium-filled balloon, which had escaped from the youth group's party the night before, started settling behind the pastor. The smiley face on the balloon was just a bit inappropriate for the sermon topic.

M.T., AR

Did you know that . . .

The so-called "Wicked Bible" (London, 1631), dropped a crucial "not," so that the commandment read, "Thou shalt commit adultery." The publisher was fined three thousand pounds.

The "Vinegar Bible" (Oxford, 1716) substituted "vinegar" for "vineyard" in Luke 22:9.

The "Wife-Hater Bible" (Oxford, 1810) had Jesus saying in Luke 13:26, "If any man come to me and hate not his own wife also, he cannot be my disciple."

Excuses People Give for Not Going to Church

It's easier to watch what's-his-name on TV.

We went last week.

93

I knew the pastor in college.

My ex-wife goes there.

My ex-husband goes there.

I haven't sinned much lately.

It makes lunch late.

I can't stand crying babies.

Sitting on pews hurts my hemorrhoids.

The bridge was out.

Turning the songbook pages makes my fingers tired.

We didn't want to walk in late, so we didn't go at all.

It exhausts me.

It's none of your business. What are you doing, writing a book?

✝

Isn't there a Bible verse that says, "Lighten up"?

Ken Alley grew up a preacher's kid in the South and Midwest. He lives with his wife, Mary, in York, Nebraska, where he combines a chiropractic career with regular churchgoing and the pursuit of discovering the humor in all kinds of real-life circumstances. Ken and Mary have three children.

Ken is available for speaking engagements to all churches and religious, civic, family and other organizations. His topic is "A Lighter Look at Human Nature (Funny Things That Happen to Real People)." To contact him for speaking or to send him stories, write P.O. Box 552, York, Nebraska 68467.